Crochet Patterns for Your Dog: Beautiful and Easy to Follow Clothes and Accessories to Craft for Your Loyal Loved Ones

Disclaimer and Terms of Use: Effort has been made to ensure that the information in this book is accurate and complete, however, the author and the publisher do not warrant the accuracy of the information, text and graphics contained within the book due to the rapidly changing nature of science, research, known and unknown facts and internet. The Author and the publisher do not hold any responsibility for errors, omissions or contrary interpretation of the subject matter herein. This book is presented solely for motivational and informational purposes only.

TABLE OF CONTENTS

PREFACE

So you have successfully coated the entire contents of your house in crochet projects, everything from the bathroom to the kitchen has some sort of yarn related accessory, now you feel like you need to fulfill your crochet addiction another way.

Fear not! This handy little eBook will teach you everything you need to know to finally coat your fluffy friends in layers upon layers of crochet goodies! No dog will be safe from your crochet skills!

In this guide you will find helpful tutorials on creating pet beds to compliment any room, how to turn your puppy into a superhero and you will even find a variety of different coats and sweaters to suit any breed.

So what are you waiting for? Grab your hook, yarn and potentially unwilling dog and get crocheting!

CROCHET DOG BANDANA

Dressing your dog's up in bandanas, either as an accessory or to use as a functional collar is popular all over the world, this pattern allows you to customize your dog's bandana to suit their personality and breed. This simple pattern takes very little yarn which allows you to make it from leftover balls, plus it takes hardly any time to make and contains basic crochet terms, this makes this project very beginner friendly.

This crochet bandana is useful just as an accessory but not as an actual collar due to how yarn tends to stretch after a while, you can either tie this around your dog like a proper bandana or use a Velcro closure if you feel that you would like to get it off more easily.

This pattern is for a medium sized dog, it is suitable for breeds such as spaniels, Labradors and bulldogs, you can easily make this bigger or smaller by increasing or decreasing the starting chain as it won't interfere with the pattern.

Things you will need:

- 1 ball of DK (8 ply) yarn in the color of your choice, this pattern is for a plain bandana but you can easily makes yours multicolored if you wish.
- A 4mm crochet hook
- Tapestry needle
- Scissors
- Velcro (optional)

Row 1: Start off by chaining 51, (you can make this number larger or smaller depending on the size of the dog) dc into the 2nd ch from the hook and into the remaining 49 chains, ch 2 and turn your work (50)

Row 2: Decrease (dc2tog) over the first 2 stitches, put 1 dc into the next 46 stitches and decrease in the last 2 stitches remaining, ch 2 and turn your work (48)

Row 3: Decrease (dc2tog) over the first 2 stitches, put 1 dc into the next 44 stitches and decrease in the last 2 stitches remaining, ch 2 and turn your work (46)

Row 4: Decrease (dc2tog) over the first 2 stitches, put 1 dc into the next 42 stitches and decrease in the last 2 stitches remaining, ch 2 and turn your work (44)

Row 5: Decrease (dc2tog) over the first 2 stitches, put 1 dc into the next 40 stitches and decrease in the last 2 stitches remaining, ch 2 and turn your work (42)

Row 6: Decrease (dc2tog) over the first 2 stitches, put 1 dc into the next 38 stitches and decrease in the last 2 stitches remaining, ch 2 and turn your work (40)

Row 7: Decrease (dc2tog) over the first 2 stitches, put 1 dc into the next 36 stitches and decrease in the last 2 stitches remaining, ch 2 and turn your work (38)

Row 8: Decrease (dc2tog) over the first 2 stitches, put 1 dc into the next 34 stitches and decrease in the last 2 stitches remaining, ch 2 and turn your work (36)

Row 9: Decrease (dc2tog) over the first 2 stitches, put 1 dc into the next 32 stitches and decrease in the last 2 stitches remaining, ch 2 and turn your work (34)

Row 10: Decrease (dc2tog) over the first 2 stitches, put 1 dc into the next 30 stitches and decrease in the last 2 stitches remaining, ch 2 and turn your work (32)

Row 11: Decrease (dc2tog) over the first 2 stitches, put 1 dc into the next 28 stitches and decrease in the last 2 stitches remaining, ch 2 and turn your work (30)

Row 12: Decrease (dc2tog) over the first 2 stitches, put 1 dc into the next 26 stitches and decrease in the last 2 stitches remaining, ch 2 and turn your work (28)

Row 13: Decrease (dc2tog) over the first 2 stitches, put 1 dc into the next 24 stitches and decrease in the last 2 stitches remaining, ch 2 and turn your work (26)

Row 14: Decrease (dc2tog) over the first 2 stitches, put 1 dc into the next 22 stitches and decrease in the last 2 stitches remaining, ch 2 and turn your work (24)

Row 15: Decrease (dc2tog) over the first 2 stitches, put 1 dc into the next 20 stitches and decrease in the last 2 stitches remaining, ch 2 and turn your work (22)

Row 16: Decrease (dc2tog) over the first 2 stitches, put 1 dc into the next 18 stitches and decrease in the last 2 stitches remaining, ch 2 and turn your work (20)

Row 17: Decrease (dc2tog) over the first 2 stitches, put 1 dc into the next 16 stitches and decrease in the last 2 stitches remaining, ch 2 and turn your work (18)

Row 18: Decrease (dc2tog) over the first 2 stitches, put 1 dc into the next 14 stitches and decrease in the last 2 stitches remaining, ch 2 and turn your work (16)

Row 19: Decrease (dc2tog) over the first 2 stitches, put 1 dc into the next 12 stitches and decrease in the last 2 stitches remaining, ch 2 and turn your work (14)

Row 20: Decrease (dc2tog) over the first 2 stitches, put 1 dc into the next 10 stitches and decrease in the last 2 stitches remaining, ch 2 and turn your work (12)

Row 21: Decrease (dc2tog) over the first 2 stitches, put 1 dc into the next 8 stitches and decrease in the last 2 stitches remaining, ch 2 and turn your work (10)

Row 22: Decrease (dc2tog) over the first 2 stitches, put 1 dc into the next 6 stitches and decrease in the last 2 stitches remaining, ch 2 and turn your work (8)

Row 23: Decrease (dc2tog) over the first 2 stitches, put 1 dc into the next 4 stitches and decrease in the last 2 stitches remaining, ch 2 and turn your work (6)

Row 24: Decrease (dc2tog) over the first 2 stitches, put 1 dc into the next 2 stitches and decrease in the last 2 stitches remaining, ch 2 and turn your work (4)

Row 25: Decrease over the remaining 4 stitches to finish off the bandana in a nice point.

Finish off and weave in any loose ends with a tapestry needle, at this point you can easily start using the bandana, if you would like you can attach a small bit of Velcro to the ends to make it easier to take it on and off the dog.

SMASH PROOF INDOOR PLAY BALL

One of the most destructive things about owning a dog is the need to play in the house, now usually this is no problem but sooner or later something is going to break or the dog chewing on a squeaky toy at 3am is enough to make you go mad, this handy soft ball not only stops things from being broken but it also mutes any noise (unless you choose to put a squeaky toy in it!)

This pattern is worked in continuous rounds; this means that you will not join your work at any point unless specified, when you come to the end of a round, instead of joining you will simply just work on top of the stitches from the previous round, this gives you a nice clean look with no seam.

Things you will need:

- 1 ball of worsted weight yarn in the color of your choice
- A 4mm crochet hook
- Tapestry needle
- Scissors
- Toy filler
- A small dog ball, around the size of a tennis ball, you can also make it squeaky if you choose
- Stitch markers

Rnd 1: Start off with a magic loop, put 6 sc into the loop and tighten it to create a small circle (6)

Rnd 2: Put 2 sc into each stitch in the round (12)

Rnd 3: *Put 1 sc into the first stitch, put 2 single crochets into the following stitch* repeat from *to* until you reach the end of the round (18)

After round 3, insert a stitch marker into the yarn so you know where the beginnings of your rounds are and to help you count your rows.

Rnd 4: *Put 1 sc into the first 2 stitches, put 2 single crochets into the following stitch* repeat from *to* until you reach the end of the round (24)

Rnd 5: *Put 1 sc into the first 3 stitches, put 2 single crochets into the following stitch* repeat from *to* until you reach the end of the round (30)

Rnd 6: *Put 1 sc into the first 4 stitches, put 2 single crochets into the following stitch* repeat from *to* until you reach the end of the round (36)

Rnd 7: *Put 1 sc into the first 5 stitches, put 2 single crochets into the following stitch* repeat from *to* until you reach the end of the round (42)

Rnd 8: *Put 1 sc into the first 6 stitches, put 2 single crochets into the following stitch* repeat from *to* until you reach the end of the round (48)

Rnd 9: *Put 1 sc into the first 7 stitches, put 2 single crochets into the following stitch* repeat from *to* until you reach the end of the round (54)

Rnd 10: Put 1 sc into each stitch in the round (54)

Rnd 11: *Put 1 sc into the first 6 stitches, sc2tog in the next 2 stitches* repeat from *to* until you reach the end of the round (48)

Rnd 12: *Put 1 sc into the first 5 stitches, sc2tog in the next 2 stitches* repeat from *to* until you reach the end of the round (42)

At this point in time you will want to start stuffing the cavity full of toy filler, try and focus the filler around the sides and bottom of the ball building up a thick layer, next place the small tennis ball or other squeaky toy into the center of the ball and then surround it with toy filler.

Rnd 13: *Put 1 sc into the first 4 stitches, sc2tog in the next 2 stitches* repeat from *to* until you reach the end of the round (36)

Rnd 14: *Put 1 sc into the first 3 stitches, sc2tog in the next 2 stitches* repeat from *to* until you reach the end of the round (30)

Rnd 15: *Put 1 sc into the first 2 stitches, sc2tog in the next 2 stitches* repeat from *to* until you reach the end of the round (24)

Put any last amounts of stuffing into the ball at this point in time as you won't be able to after the next step.

Rnd 16: *Put 1 sc into the first stitch, sc2tog in the next 2 stitches* repeat from *to* until you reach the end of the round (18)

Rnd 17: Sc2tog all the way around the round to close up the remaining hole.

Finish off and use a tapestry needle to sew closed the remaining hole then it is all ready to be used by your fluffy friend!

Cozy Pet Bed

This pet bed pattern is incredibly versatile, whether you are making it for your new puppy or making it to give to a charity, there will always be a dog that finds comfort in this lovely round padded bed.

This pattern is suitable either for younger dogs or for smaller breeds such as little Terriers, Whippets and mixed breeds, to make this bed bigger simply carry on with the increasing rows to increase the size of the circle.

It is advised that you use a synthetic yarn or something that can withstand the washing machine without losing its shape; chunky yarns such as Aran yarn or chunky synthetic are perfect for this.

Things you will need:

- 3 balls of chunky or bulky (12 ply) yarn in the colors of your choice
- A 6mm crochet hook
- Tapestry needle
- Scissors
- Toy filler
- A small pad or pillow to go in the center of the bed

Rnd 1: Begin by making a magic loop with your yarn, put 6 hdc in the loop and tighten it to form a small circle, join with a sl st and ch 2 (6)

Rnd 2: Put 2 hdc into every stitch in the round, join up with a sl st and ch 2 (12)

Rnd 3: *Put 1 hdc into the first stitch, put 2 hdc into the following stitch* repeat from *to* all the way around until you reach the end, join with a sl st and ch 2 (18)

Rnd 4: *Put 1 hdc into the first 2 stitches, put 2 hdc into the following stitch* repeat from *to* all the way around until you reach the end, join with a sl st and ch 2 (24)

Rnd 5: *Put 1 hdc into the first 3 stitches, put 2 hdc into the following stitch* repeat from *to* all the way around until you reach the end, join with a sl st and ch 2 (30)

Rnd 6: *Put 1 hdc into the first 4 stitches, put 2 hdc into the following stitch* repeat from *to* all the way around until you reach the end, join with a sl st and ch 2 (36)

Rnd 7: *Put 1 hdc into the first 5 stitches, put 2 hdc into the following stitch* repeat from *to* all the way around until you reach the end, join with a sl st and ch 2 (42)

Rnd 8: *Put 1 hdc into the first 6 stitches, put 2 hdc into the following stitch* repeat from *to* all the way around until you reach the end, join with a sl st and ch 2 (48)

Rnd 9: *Put 1 hdc into the first 7 stitches, put 2 hdc into the following stitch* repeat from *to* all the way around until you reach the end, join with a sl st and ch 2 (54)

Rnd 10: *Put 1 hdc into the first 8 stitches, put 2 hdc into the following stitch* repeat from *to* all the way around until you reach the end, join with a sl st and ch 2 (60)

Rnd 11: *Put 1 hdc into the first 9 stitches, put 2 hdc into the following stitch* repeat from *to* all the way around until you reach the end, join with a sl st and ch 2 (66)

Rnd 12: *Put 1 hdc into the first 10 stitches, put 2 hdc into the following stitch* repeat from *to* all the way around until you reach the end, join with a sl st and ch 2 (72)

Rnd 13-18: Put 1 hdc into each stitch in the round, join with a sl st and ch 2, after a couple of rounds the corners should begin to fold upwards and inwards (72)

Rnd 19-20: Put 1 hdc into each stitch in the round, make sure to use a higher tension to tighten up the last 2 rows to make the bed easier to assemble, join with a sl st and ch 2 (72)

Finish off and weave in any loose ends with a tapestry needle.

Assembly:

To put together the pet bed, grab a tapestry needle and a long bit of yarn.

You want to begin folding in the sides of the bed to form a small rounded lip to the bed to stop the dog from rolling out accidently, you want to roughly fold the bed in about 10 rounds worth, use pins to hold the edges in this position then begin sewing around.

Make sure to stop every 5 inches or so and insert the toy filler, make sure to pack it in tightly to make the bed springy.

Continue in this fashion all the way around the bed until you reach the end, you may want to run another row of stitches around the edges to keep any stuffing from coming out, now all that is left to do is to put a pad or pillow in the very center of the bed to make it extra comfy for your fluffy friend!

EASY CROCHET DOG MUZZLE

Muzzles are a great training item to be used for noise control and behaviour issues in dogs, these muzzles are not meant to be used for stopping a dog from biting or attacking other animals, it is more to be used for a barking deterrent or to give better control in training situations; it is not recommended that this muzzle be used to prevent biting.

These muzzles are soft and non-harmful to the dog, they are made out of very little yarn and can be made in under an hour due to the shortness of the project, and these make fantastic gifts or can simply be made for your own pets.

The below pattern is suitable for a medium to large sized dog breeds like Labradors, German Shepherds and Huskies, it is however very easy to alter for smaller or larger breeds.

Things you will need:

- 1 ball of strong and chunky worsted weight yarn in the color of your choice
- A 5mm crochet hook
- Tapestry needle
- Scissors
- Measuring tape

You will start by crocheting the band that will go around the muzzle

Row 1: Begin by chaining 11, hdc into the 2nd ch from the hook and into the remaining 9 chains, ch 2 and turn your work (10)

Row 2: Put 1 hdc into every stitch in the row, once you reach the end ch 2 and turn.

Row 3-8: Put 1 hdc into every stitch in the row, once you reach the end ch 2 and turn.

You don't want the muzzle to be a really tight fit but it needs to be quite snug to deter barking, test it on your dog to see if it is tight enough for this, you can add or take away rows.

Once you have finished your rows, bring the 2 ends together and either slip stitch or sew the ends securely together.

Now you want to create the band that holds the muzzle to the dogs' head, to do this you will want to create a chain long enough that fits quite tightly to the back of the head.

Begin by chaining 15; this number can be altered higher or lower depending on the width of the dogs head.

Hdc into the 2nd ch from the hook and into the remaining 13 chains, once you reach the end, chain 2 and turn your work then hdc into every stitch in the row.

Once you come to the end, finish off and weave in loose ends with a tapestry needle.

To put the muzzle together, take the band you have just created and line up each end on either side of the muzzle where the dogs mouth and nose will sit, sew the band to the muzzle using a tapestry needle, make sure this is secure to stop any breaking.

Once the band is sewn on, simply secure the yarn and weave in any loose end then you are ready to start using the muzzle right away!

This pattern is only a rough universal pattern and you may need to adjust certain aspects such as the band or muzzle length to make it suitable for individual dogs.

GRANNY SQUARE DOG COAT

This fun pattern is perfect for little dogs that feel the cold more than others, especially in the winter months! This coat is designed to be beginner friendly by using a basic granny square pattern and bringing loads of little squares together to fit most sizes of dog.

The below pattern is designed to fit most small to medium toy breeds of dog, this includes breeds like poodles, schnauzers etc. to increase the size of the coat to fit bigger dogs you will need to add more granny squares accordingly.

Things you will need:

- 2-3 balls of DK (8 ply) or worsted weight yarn in the color of your choice.
- A 4mm crochet hook (use a 5mm if making this for bigger dogs)
- Tapestry needle
- Scissors
- Measuring tape
- Velcro strips

To make the granny squares:

Rnd 1: Start off by forming a magic loop, within the loop ch 3, this ch 3 is present in every row and will always count as a dc, next to your ch 3 put 2 dc, *then ch 2 and put 3 more dc* repeat from *to* until you have 4 sets of 3 dc, ch 2 and sl st through the top of your ch 3 to join.

You will now be working in spaces rather than stitches; this means all of your stitches will now sit in the ch 2 spaces you create in every round.

Rnd 2: Begin with a ch 3 (counts as 1 dc), put 2 dc in the corner space along with your ch 3, *ch 2 and move into the next corner space, in this space put 3 dc, ch 2 and a final 3 dc* repeat from *to* until you have filled all 3 corners, in the final corner where you started, put 3 dc and a ch 2 before joining with a sl st to the top of your ch 3.

Rnd 3: Begin with a ch 3 (counts as 1 dc), put 2 dc in the corner space along with your ch 3, *ch 2 and move into the ch 2 space in the middle of the row, put 3 dc here and ch 2 before moving into the corner space, in this space put 3 dc, ch 2 and a final 3 dc* repeat from *to* until you have filled all 3 sides, in the final corner where you started, put 3 dc and a ch 2 before joining with a sl st to the top of your ch 3.

Rnd 4: Begin with a ch 3 (counts as 1 dc), put 2 dc in the corner space along with your ch 3, *ch 2 and move into the ch 2 space in the middle of the row, put 3 dc here and ch 2, move into the next ch 2 space and do another 3 dc and ch 2 before moving into the corner space, in this space put 3 dc, ch 2 and a final 3 dc* repeat from *to* until you have filled all 3 sides, in the final corner where you started, put 3 dc and a ch 2 before joining with a sl st to the top of your ch 3.

Finish off and weave in ends with a tapestry needle.

Assembly:

To put the coat together, you will need a total of 16 granny squares (this increases the bigger you make it).

Take 9 of your granny squares and line them up so that they form a 3x3 grid, take a tapestry needle and some yarn and sew all of these panels together by whip stitching them all together to form one solid sheet of granny squares.

Next take 2 granny squares sew one to the top right hand corner of the coat (so it lines up with the square below it) and sew one to the top left hand corner.

Take 2 more squares and sew them to the ends of the 2 squares you have just attached, you should now have a 3x3 grid of squares with 2 squares protruding from the left and right top corners, and these two protrusions will form the neck hole.

Next take 2 more squares, sew the first one to the middle of the left hand side of your 3x3 grid and sew the other to the middle of the right hand side of your grid, with you last remaining square, attach it to one of the squares you have just attached to the coat, this will form the strip that wraps around the dogs belly.

Now taking a needle and thread or a hot glue gun, attach a 1 inch strip of Velcro to both the inner corners of the neck hole and the middle edge of the chest strips.

Finish off and weave in any loose ends left over from assembly with a tapestry needle then you are ready to dress your dog up in a nice warm coat!

DOG SOCKS

Just like humans, dogs can also suffer with cold feet too, if an owner isn't careful in winter months their dogs can indeed end up getting frost bitten paws which can end up being a hefty vet bill, these dog socks are perfect for keeping little dogs paws all nice and warm when the weather turns chilly.

These dog socks are made out of very little yarn and come together very quickly with one sock taking approximately half an hour to make, you can make them all in one color or all in different colors depending on your preference.

Things you will need:

- 1 ball of DK (8 ply) yarn in the color of your choice
- A 4mm crochet hook
- Tapestry needle
- Scissors
- 4 1cm thick strips of elastic big enough o fit comfortably around your dog's paws
- Small needle and thread

Rnd 1: Start off by making a magic loop, put 6 hdc within the loop and tighten it up so it forms a little circle, join with a sl st and ch 2 (6)

Rnd 2: Put 2 hdc within each of the 6 stitches in the round, join with a sl st and ch 2 (12)

Rnd 3: *Put 1 hdc into the first stitch, put 2 stitches into the following stitch* (18)

At this point, check to see if the circle you have formed will fit the bottom of your dog's paw, if they are too small add another round using the following formula: *Put 1 hdc into the first 2 stitches, put 2 stitches into the following stitch*, if the circle is too big then remove a round then check to see if it fits.

Rnd 4: Put 1 sc into each stitch in the round in the back loop only, this will form a bend which will help shape the sock over the dogs' foot.

Rnd 5: Put 1 hdc into each of the stitches in the round, join with a sl st and ch 2 (18)

Rnd 6-12: Put 1 hdc into each of the stitches in the round, join with a sl st and ch 2 (18)

Once complete, check to see if the dogs paws will sit comfortably within the socks, you may need to add more rows if the socks do not go up high enough or go back and make them wider if they are too tight.

Once all the socks fit properly, put to one side for a minute while you sort out the elastic.

Next take your strips of elastic and measure them around where the socks will sit around the dogs legs and cut them all to size, they need to be tight enough to hold the sock to the leg but loose enough to not impair the animal in any way.

Once cut to size, use your needle and thread to sew an X shape into the elastic to hold it together securely, turn the socks inside out and place the elastic around the outside of the top of the sock, roll the sock down so that it covers the elastic then using a tapestry needle and yarn to sew the sock in place to hide the elastic, repeat with each of the socks before turning them the right way out again.

Finish off and weave in any loose ends left over then you are ready to keep your dog's feet warm!

Easy Dog Sweater

This simple little doggy sweater will keep your little treasures nice and warm through the colder months of the year where smaller less fluffy breeds tend to suffer a little bit when out and about, this adorable sweater is ideal for smaller breeds of dog such as toy varieties, Corgis, and Terriers, they are also suitable for puppies that are between 5-12 weeks depending on the breed.

The following pattern is created for smaller breeds in mind, if you would like a larger coat pattern, please refer to the granny square coat pattern within this guide or play around with the stitches in this pattern to get it the right size.

Things you will need:

- 1 ball of worsted weight yarn in the color of your choice
- A 4mm crochet hook
- Tapestry needle
- Scissors

Rnd 1: begin by chaining a long chain of 70, this will be going around the dogs belly, join it together with a sl st being careful that the chain doesn't twist in odd directions to form one big ring, ch 2 then put h dc into every stitch in the round, join with a sl st and ch 2.

The number of stitches per round you have in this pattern is not exact as it varies per breed; also make sure not to turn your work at the end of every round.

Rnd 2: Put 1 hdc into every stitch in the round; join with a sl st and ch 2, do not turn.

Rnd 3-10: Put 1 hdc into every stitch in the round; join with a sl st and ch 2, do not turn.

Rnd 11: Begin this round by slip stitching through the first 20 stitches, this method is used to travel through your crochet work without adding a row, ch 2 then hdc into the following 39 stitches, ch 2 and turn your work, at this point you will be creating the fabric that goes over the shoulders and no longer working in a round for now.

Rnd 12: Put 1 hdc into every hdc stitch from the previous round, ch 2 and turn your work

Rnd 13-18: Put 1 hdc into every hdc stitch from the previous round, ch 2 and turn your work

You will now form the part of the sweater that goes around the dogs' neck and begin working in a round again.

Rnd 19: Put 1 hdc into every hdc stitch from the previous round, you will now want to chain 16 and slip stitch through the first stitch in the opposite side of your row, this will form a loop so you can work in a round again and form the neck hole.

Rnd 20: Begin with a ch 2, put 1 hdc into every stitch in the round, make sure to hdc into each of the 16 chains from the previous round; join with a sl st and ch 2.

Rnd 21-22: Put 1 hdc in each stitch in the round, join with a sl st and ch 2.

Finish off and weave in any loose ends with a tapestry needle then you are all ready to warm your little fluffy friend up!

QUIRKY PUPPY BLANKET

Every puppy needs a favourite blanket; just like children they can form attachments to certain items such as toys or soft things so why shouldn't your special fluffy friend have their very own blanket to snuggle in to of a night time or to keep warm on a chilly winter's morning?

This simple but quirky pets blanket is quite a big project so it will take the best part of at least a few days to complete,

Things you will need:

- 4 balls of chunky or worsted weight yarn in the colors of your choice, it is better to use all different colors
- A 5mm crochet hook
- Tapestry needle
- Scissors

Row 1: Begin by chaining 71 with your first color, hdc into the 2nd ch from the hook and into the remaining 69 stitches, ch 2 and turn your work (70)

Row 2-4: Hdc into each stitch in the row, ch 2 and turn your work (70)

Row 5: Switch to your second color, Hdc into each stitch in the row, ch 2 and turn your work (70)

Row 6-8: Hdc into each stitch in the row, ch 2 and turn your work (70)

Row 9: Switch to your third color, Hdc into each stitch in the row, ch 2 and turn your work (70)

Row 10-12: Hdc into each stitch in the row, ch 2 and turn your work (70)

Row 13: Switch to your fourth color, Hdc into each stitch in the row, ch 2 and turn your work (70)

Row 14-16: Hdc into each stitch in the row, ch 2 and turn your work (70)

Row 17: Switch to your first color, Hdc into each stitch in the row, ch 2 and turn your work (70)

Row 18-20: Hdc into each stitch in the row, ch 2 and turn your work (70)

Row 21: Switch to your second color, Hdc into each stitch in the row, ch 2 and turn your work (70)

Row 22-24: Hdc into each stitch in the row, ch 2 and turn your work (70)

Row 25: Switch to your third color, Hdc into each stitch in the row, ch 2 and turn your work (70)

Row 26-28: Hdc into each stitch in the row, ch 2 and turn your work (70)

Row 29: Switch to your fourth color, Hdc into each stitch in the row, ch 2 and turn your work (70)

Row 30-32: Hdc into each stitch in the row, ch 2 and turn your work (70)

At this point if the blanket is big enough then you can easily repeat rows 17-32 to increase the blanket by another block of colors, if the blanket is big enough then simply finish off in your usual fashion and weave in any loose ends with a tapestry needle.

To give the blanket a nice, clean and professional looking effect, pick one of your 4 colors and attach the yarn to the outside of the blanket, run a row of single crochet around the entire edge of the blanket making sure to put 4 single crochet stitches in the corner to avoid the blanket curling in on itself.

SUPERHERO CAPE

This adorable and quick little pattern can turn even the smallest of dogs into a canine crime fighter! This cute little dog cape is designed especially for little dogs to make them feel as tall as a Great Dane and as mighty as an Alaskan malamute!

This simple little project can take a little while due to the use of single crochet, if you would like to make this for a bigger dog then simply increase the starting chain as it will not affect the pattern.

The cape is designed to tie directly to the dogs' collar with a few simple bits of yarn or if you like you can add a small strip of elastic to make removal easier, it is specially made for smaller breeds of dog such as beagles, pugs and Chihuahuas.

Things you will need:

- 1 ball of DK (8 ply) yarn in a rich red color
- A 4mm crochet hook
- Tapestry needle
- Scissors
- Small strip of elastic the same length as your dog's neck so it isn't too tight

Row 1: Start by chaining 21, sc into the 2nd ch from the hook and into the remaining 19 stitches, ch 1 and turn your work (20)

Row 2-4: Put 1 sc into every stitch in the row, ch 1 and turn your work (20)

This small little section you have just created will form the housing for the elastic.

Row 5: Put 2 sc into the first stitch of the row, 1 sc into the next 18 stitches, put 2 sc into the last stitch of the row, ch 1 and turn your work (22)

Row 6: Put 2 sc into the first stitch of the row, 1 sc into the next 20 stitches, put 2 sc into the last stitch of the row, ch 1 and turn your work (24)

Row 7: Put 2 sc into the first stitch of the row, 1 sc into the next 22 stitches, put 2 sc into the last stitch of the row, ch 1 and turn your work (26)

Row 8: Put 2 sc into the first stitch of the row, 1 sc into the next 24 stitches, put 2 sc into the last stitch of the row, ch 1 and turn your work (28)

Row 9: Put 2 sc into the first stitch of the row, 1 sc into the next 26 stitches, put 2 sc into the last stitch of the row, ch 1 and turn your work (30)

Row 10: Put 2 sc into the first stitch of the row, 1 sc into the next 28 stitches, put 2 sc into the last stitch of the row, ch 1 and turn your work (32)

Row 11: Put 2 sc into the first stitch of the row, 1 sc into the next 30 stitches, put 2 sc into the last stitch of the row, ch 1 and turn your work (34)

Row 12: Put 2 sc into the first stitch of the row, 1 sc into the next 32 stitches, put 2 sc into the last stitch of the row, ch 1 and turn your work (36)

Row 13-20: Put 1 sc into every stitch in the round, ch 1 and turn your work (36)

Finish off and weave in any loose ends with a tapestry needle.

To complete the cape, take your elastic and place it over the 20 stitch long section you created at the beginning of the cape, fold over the flap to hold the elastic then whip stitch with a tapestry needle to hold it in place, finally sew the elastic together securely and you're ready to start making your dog feel like a superhero!

WOVEN EFFECT DOG COLLAR

One of the main ways an owner will help to express a dog's personality is through their collars, the problem is that collars these days are ridiculously expensive and you can spend an absolute fortune on a good quality collar.

These crochet collars, although not functional, are a great way of customizing how your animal looks without spending out on loads of different collars for different occasions, these stretchy collars fit over the top of an existing collar to allow you to clip your lead onto the rings on the collar underneath and still have to crochet collar on top.

They require very little yarn and hardly take any time to complete making this the perfect quick little project for a lazy afternoon; these also make great gifts for anyone getting a new dog, this collar cover is perfect for a larger dog, however you can easily make this smaller by adjusting the pattern slightly.

Things you will need:

- 1 ball of worsted weight yarn in the color of your choice
- A 5mm crochet hook
- Tapestry needle
- Scissors

This pattern is worked by creating a couple different layers of yarn before intertwining them to create the finished product.

Row 1: Begin by chaining 6, hdc into the 2nd ch from the hook and hdc into the remaining chains in the row, ch 2 and turn your work (5)

Row 2: Hdc into each of the stitches in the row, ch 2 and turn your work (5)

Row 3-20 (it should be longer than the width of your dog's neck as it will shrink when assembled): Hdc into each of the stitches in the row, ch 2 and turn your work (5)

To finish off, sc around the entire strand to give it a nice border, weave in any loose ends with a tapestry needle then set aside.

To continue, repeat rows 1 to 21 until you have a total of 3 strands, you can also make 4-5 strands depending on your braiding knowledge.

Once you have all of your 3 strands complete, lay one on top of the other and put a single stitch with a tapestry needle at the very end of the strips just to hold them all on top of each other.

Next get someone to help you for this next part! Get them to pinch the end where you put a stitch and pull gently to give the yarn some tension.

Taking your 3 strands, tightly braid them together to form one cohesive piece of yarn, don't worry if it looks a little messy you can tidy that up in a second.

Next, line the strands up with the beginning of the row, either get someone to sew them for you or use a tapestry needle to sew all of the strands together to form one big loop and a collar.

To use this collar simply put it over the top of your dog's regular collar to conceal it and help bring a bit of color to your animals personality.

BOWL MATS

These handy bowl mats are great for keeping your floor free from water spills and dog food sticking to the floor, the best part about them is that they have a special grip like bottom that stops them from sliding about when the dog is eating and drinking.

This project can either be made smaller for individual bowls or you can follow the pattern below to make a larger mat to hold water and food bowls, this project requires roughly 1 ball of yarn and takes a fair time to make due to the number of rows making this the perfect lazy day project.

Things you will need:

- 1 ball of Aran or chunky yarn in the color of your choice
- 1 ball of Aran or chunky yarn in a different color for the border
- A 5mm crochet hook
- Tapestry needle
- Scissors
- Hot glue gun & glue sticks

Row 1: Start off by chaining 42, hdc into the 2nd ch from the hook and into the remaining 39 chains, when you reach the end ch 2 and turn your work (40)

Row 2: Hdc into every stitch in the row, once you reach the end ch 2 and turn your work (40)

Row 3-20: Hdc into every stitch in the row, once you reach the end ch 2 and turn your work (40)

Once you finish the main mat, place it down and see if the bowls both fit nicely onto the allocated space, if not you can add more rows to make it wider or go back and increase the starting number in your chain.

Row 21: Switch over to your second color of yarn and attach it to one of the corners on the mat, put a sc into every stitch around the outside of the mat, make sure to put 3 sc into the corners to stop it from rolling in on itself, join with a sl st.

At this point you can choose to leave it as it is by finishing off and weaving in loose ends or you can add a nice row of shell stitches around the edges, to do this you need to be starting in a corner.

In the corner put *2 dc, a ch 2 then a final 2 dc to form a shell stitch, you will then want to skip 2 stitches* and repeat from *to* all the way around the border of your mat making sure the shell stitches always end up in the corner spaces.

Once complete, join with a simple sl st and finish off then use a tapestry needle to weave in any loose ends you may have.

Now take your hot glue gun and glue sticks to add the grips to the bottom, essentially what you want to do once the glue gun has warmed up is place a 1 cm sized blob of glue at every inch spacing across the mat. Then move up an inch and repeat the same process again but this time make sure your blobs are off center from the first row, repeat in this fashion all the way up the mat, make sure to not put the glue dots on the shell edging at it will not stick due to the stitches being more spread out, once you reach the end, allow the glue to set for an hour or so then the mat is ready to use!

Puppy Ear Warmers

Now I know what you're thinking, how can you make ear warmers for a dog? Actually it is surprisingly easy with this simple to do pattern! This easy pair of ear warmers means that your dog's sensitive little ears won't freeze when the wind is cold and can also prevent ear infections.

The finished effect is very similar to a snood which many women wear today in modern fashion; it is designed to be almost like a tube that fits over your dog's head with Velcro strips for easy removal.

The pattern below is suitable for medium sized dogs but it does stretch quite a lot, you will want this to fit snuggly around the dogs head without impairing their breathing or being too uncomfortable, to adjust this pattern simply take or add from the beginning chain as it doesn't affect the overall pattern.

Things you will need:

- 1 ball of worsted weight yarn in the color of your choice
- A 4.5mm crochet hook
- Tapestry needle
- Scissors
- Needle and thread
- 2 x 1 inch strips of Velcro

Row 1: Begin by chaining 15, this should be long enough to cover your dog's ear as well as part of the forehead and neck, if this is too long then reduce the number of chains, if it isn't long enough then add more chains until it does, hdc into the 2nd ch from the hook and into the remaining stitches in the row, ch 2 and turn your work (14)

Row 2: Hdc into each of the stitches in the row in the back loop only, ch 2 and turn your work (14)

Row 3-20: Hdc into each of the stitches in the row in the back loop only, ch 2 and turn your work (14)

The 20 rows should be enough to stretch around the dogs head, if it is too small or too big, adjust the number of rows accordingly.

Once your rectangle is complete, finish off and weave in any loose ends with a tapestry needle.

Take your needle and thread, line up your strips of Velcro on the very ends of the rectangle so that when folded over they will stick together, pin in place before sewing securely to the yarn to keep it in place.

To use this ear warmer, wrap it around your dog's head making sure to tuck their ears down and back so that they are comfortable, bring the 2 ends of the ear warmer together and use the Velcro strips to secure the ear warmer in place.

These ear warmers are perfect for walks outdoors or chilly days, prolonged wearing of the ear warmer is not advised as it can cause wax build up within the dog's ears and impair their hearing, as such do not let your dog off the leash with this on its head.

STITCH ABBREVIATIONS & SELF HELP SECTION

This chapter is designed to help you whenever you become stuck at any point throughout this eBook, if there is a question about terminology or crochet hook that you have, you will find it here!

Here you will find a terminology chart to help you understand the abbreviated words within the text, a conversion chart between US and UK terminology to help you with patterns outside of this guide as well as a handy crochet hook conversion chart to help you find the right hook size.

US AND UK TERMINOLOGY

Although most crochet terms are universal around the world, the terms can vary ever so slightly between the US and the UK, the chart below indicates these changes in case you find yourself using a UK based pattern and are confused as to why your crocheting doesn't look the same.

US Terminology	UK Equivalent
Single crochet	Double crochet
Double crochet	Treble crochet

Half double crochet	Half treble crochet
Treble crochet	Double treble crochet

CROCHET TERMINOLOGY CHART

Please use the table below to find out the meaning of the abbreviated terms within this guide.

Crochet Terminology	Abbreviation
Slip Stitch	SS or Sl St
Chain	Ch
Single Crochet	Sc
Single Crochet Two Together	sc2tog
Double Crochet Two Together	Dc2tog
Increasing	Inc
Decreasing	Dec
Back Loop Only	BLO
Double Crochet	Dc
Half Double Crochet	Hdc
Repeat	Rep
Millimeter	Mm
Stitch	St
Alternate	Alt
Treble Crochet	Tr
**	Repeat as instructed
Continue	Cont.

CROCHET HOOK CONVERSION CHART

All crochet hooks are the same, however how they are know is different around the world, they can be known either as a letter or a number although the sizes do not change, the chart below will help you work out what size crochet hook you require for your project.

Metric Sizing – Hook Size In mm	US Standard Sizing
2.0	-
2.25	1/B
2.5	-
2.75	C
3.0	-
3.25	D
3.5	4/E
3.75	F
4.0	6/G
4.5	7
5.0	8/H
5.5	9/I
6.0	10/J
6.5	10.5/K
7.0	-
8.0	11/L
9.0	13/M
10.0	15/N

CONCLUSION

At the end of this eBook you should have now successfully dressed and accessorized your fluffy friends to the best of your ability, remember to always love your pets and do what is best for them, of course there are certain patterns in this eBook that aren't exactly practical and some that are downright silly, there will be times when your dog decides to protest against the lovely multicolored sweater you have made them and may seem a little ungrateful for you effort.

Remember to shower your canines with bundles of love and reassure them with treats and cuddles and they will love whatever you make for them, crochet is always about relaxing and having fun with it, what better way to accomplish this then to make things for man's best friend!

"When the Man waked up he said, 'What is Wild Dog doing here?' And the Woman said, 'His name is not Wild Dog any more, but the First Friend, because he will be our friend for always and always and always.'"

—Rudyard Kipling (author, The Jungle Book)

Printed in Great Britain
by Amazon

51645620R00031